NOMBONO

Sundress Publications • Knoxville, TN

Copyright © 2021
ISBN: 978-1-951979-24-9
Library of Congress: 9781951979249
Published by Sundress Publications
www.sundresspublications.com

Editor: Akua Lezli Hope
Editorial Assistants: Anna Black, Erin Elizabeth Smith
Editorial Interns: Stephi Cham, Nikki Lyssy, Hannah Olsson, Ryleigh Wann

Colophon: This book is set in Georgia.
Cover Design: Kristen Ton
Book Design: Brynn Martin

NOMBONO

Anthology of Speculative Poetry
by BIPOC Creators
from Around the World

edited by
Akua Lezli Hope

TABLE OF CONTENTS

Editor's Note

Thank you, Sundress Publications, for this fabulous opportunity to collect and present many historically underrepresented voices in speculative poetry.

If this genre is new to you, welcome! We, homo sapiens, first inscribed speculative poetry after memorizing it and chanting/singing it, transmitting it orally. Verse was first and the poetry was what we now call speculative: Gilgamesh, *The Ramayana, the Mahabharata, The Iliad and The Odyssey, Beowulf*—our shared foundational creations were story-poems of a mythic, fantastic, and transformational nature. The poems herein move forward in that tradition—they rocket/transmute/warp speed forward.

NOMBONO means vision in Zulu. It looks like a neologism – good word-- and sounds lovely to say. It was a delight and honor to read the range of creations, and meet, through their work, the many dreaming scribes who worked to share their insights and visions.

And o! such visions and insights: from shape shifters to space travelers, from fraught and failed mortality to the divine, we are treated to domestic discoveries and cosmic insights. We meet mermaids and were-hyenas, ghosts and the reanimated dead, aliens, robots and, of course, our own imperfect selves.

While this may not hold true for all BIPOC speculative poets, in the work received there are sustained allusions to the challenges of oppression and societal denials. These concerns, a subtext for some and motive for others, are a welcome palliative, affirming the engagement (and relevance) of speculative poetry. These concerns and engagements echo speculative poetry's foundational roots as humanity's first literature. These poets are torch bearers of the first fire. Gather round, come close, and be warmed, lit, and fueled.

–Akua Lezli Hope
writing from the ancestral land of the Onöndowa'ga:'also known as the Seneca, in the southern Finger Lakes Region of New York State, August 2021.

Notes on Water

I was born in the garden of a thousand tears. My mother opened her eyes, & forth came my brothers & sisters. Soft & cool, they raced down her cheeks. Wetting the soil beneath her. I was number 1,087. My brother, 1,068 came from the middle eyelid, a rare occurrence & strayed left into her ear.

She sunk into the ocean. Green mangoes floated around her, larger than her breasts. The salt began to liquefy her skin & slowly we all became one body of water.

Ching-In Chen

Flood Fathers

in time of flooding stream   in time of darkening fire   in time of gathering
        boats

    one father leads me by hand   staircase choked with ghostly desire

      one father already whispers trapped in front parlor   hung in doorway like
a slaughtered pig

      I climb with difficult breathing   fleeing into open sea

    with others who you haven't said hello   with others who can see your painted
        head

you're only now beginning to know their names

Jennifer Perrine

Build

They built a bower. We were not allowed to rest
in its shade. We built a tower that loomed over
their crops. Sun-starved, they built a machine, planted it
in our fields, painted it green so we would not see
it snatching our feasts from beneath our feet. We built
a god that hooked its jaws through their children. They built
a new universe. We watched them go, built gardens
in their ruins. We grew restless, built a rocket.
Inside, we travel across galaxies looking
for their land. We build each day new ways to make them
come home. We build up our hopes that this time they'll stay.

Laura Villareal

Origin of the Starchild's Skull

Coyolxauhqui grabs a comet by its tail,

wraps it around the bellhop's throat,

loops it in

  & out, pulls it tight

into a necktie & says:

  "The moon won't push itself across the sky."

The bellhop follows her around the universe

  trolleying her baggage on a brass birdcage cart.

When the starchildren ask about her bags,

their parents tell them:

    Coyolxauhqui eats bad starchildren. She grinds

     their bones into stardust

      & keeps it in her bags."

So night after night

the starchildren dare one another

  to touch the bags.

When they reach them,

the bellhop slaps their hands,

    shakes his head, & says:

        "You must swear a blood oath

            if you want to take a peek."

They simply giggle,

    glowing brighter than

        the city lights below,

before running away to finish playing

    hopscotch in the meteor bramble.

Coyolxauhqui loves the starchildren's jingling

laughter & gives the bellhop konpeito

    to offer them for their naïve courage.

The starchildren play this game nightly until

one night a child runs

    toward the birdcage cart, giggling.

As always, the bellhop prepares to catch her

before she reaches it,

    but she trips over a comet's tail.

She stumbles, falls,

& her throat lands on the sickle edge

   of the crescent moon, decapitating her.

Light shoots away

   from her head,

   without it her skull is no longer

      able to defy gravity.

Coyolxauhqui tries to catch it, but it's too late.

The starchild's skull

                  falls

            &

                  falls

                        until it lands in Mexico.

Ellen Huang

Out of Sheol and Styx

Magma, lava, structures, ash
Sewers of blood up to my ankles
Remnants of everything.

Darkness, screeching, corpses in the walls,
Demons, blinded angels, blurred faces
Drowned voices, drowning each other out
forever in animalistic greed
Coins ripped out from beggars and offered to
gods of bloodlust and anguish
Everlasting thirst and stench of death—
Everlasting, my Palm Sunday ass.

I knit them back together at a touch
Flesh resurrected over dust and bones
I take their stolen hearts, pulsing, place
them back, and they can see, they can
see me. I take the shades, the shadows,
the hopelessness
Gather the lost like little chicks, chaotic
Take them back to the light, in this place.

Claws and teeth of this place rage
The battle is a smaller eternity, and one
that eats itself.

Then I lift my hand out of the Sheol,
out of the Styx that drips with forgetting

out of the debris of a planet without a sun
out of the earth into this morning
and the sun shines through my hand.
I think I'll keep it, pierced holes in my palms,
so they know it's me.

They will tell you this is the end of
everything, but it's not.
It's the beginning.

Russell Nichols

Blood Spatter of the Solar System

for the life

      of me

i can't tell you   where i came from.   ours
      is a history   fragmented,   the cosmic
    wreckage   of planets unformed
            or destroyed.

see: floating pieces,   bobbing
      like apples in a bath   of golden sun.
        if you can't stand   the heat,
      get out the galaxy,   they say.   or something
      like this

and like that   and like this   and i'm
   nothing   but a geological thing
      among remnants of   scattered   shrapnel, slicing
    through solar winds   that may
      or may not   be calling my name.

there is no sound   in a vacuum
    and i've been around   long enough   to know
    not to fall

for just
    any ol' celestial
            body.
        gravity   will be the end
of me
    even if

    my beginning   remains

           the darkest

             of matter.

Elsa Valmidiano

Diwata

"Some people automatically associate horns with evil. I use them to represent the outsiders or 'the others,' which is not synonymous with evil."—Camille Quintos

What if I told you She was
my goddess

and She went to bed every night
worshipping

rumpled morning sheets

    desecrated water fountains

        the crack of dinner plates

           the setting fire to a cheating man's clothes?

What if I told you Eve was our Messiah
who didn't allow

the gasping of air cradled
in sweat-soaked sheets from a bad dream

a bad life?

What if I told you Her teeth
flapped out of his skin

he, who stole from Her recluse tongue

bringing profligates to their knees?

What if I told you the Serpent was

Adam's own jealous lie?

What if I told you She breathed
roses and knives cradling Her belly?

      —how a child

could make Her body

a home
you let the lambs in to rest?

      —or when She dreamed

water so blue

the horizon became a swimming pool
between ocean and sky?

What if I told you that fire
set Her divinity ablaze

until She became the Sun itself—

Destroyer Demon Witch Woman Rebel Healer Savior Mother Maiden Matriarch
Woman Queen Warrior Woman Sin Temptress Mistress Wife Heartbreaker Lover Love
Woman   Dream   Woman   Salvation   Woman   Woman

Creator

Jamal Hodge

Loving Venus

Resplendent against the infinite dark.
Luscious beauty,
without moons.
Nothing must compete
with her luminous vanity.

Waltzing on her axis,
performative slowness,
allowing the universe
one circle
within one rotation,
of her curves.

As we orbit her seductive charms our arc reactor stalls,
tempted by our nearness,
she reaches,
dragging us,
into love.

867 degrees Fahrenheit
beneath
her yellow-white canopy, squeezing
with eager tightness
against our penetrating hull.

Ignited by her heat,
we lose ourselves
to delirium,

screaming incoherent promises
as the atmospheric pressure rises.

Computerized boosters
cannot reach escape velocity.
Crucial circuits malfunction.

We plummet at her pleasure.
 Our hull growing soft inside her,
its hardness spent.
She does not relent,
wanting more, deeper.

185 mile an hour
atmospheric winds
make satisfied howls,
her sulfuric clouds
smell of rotten eggs.

Licked by acid,
our eyes glimpse
desolate passions,
a hellish revelation of volcanos
lava, and boiling dust.

William says,
"Venus does not favor a house of tears."
She favors a house of hell.
She is hunger without relent,
a lover of bloody Mars,
bathed in toxic glory.

Our eyes escape their sockets,
oozing down flaming cheeks.
Harsh winds scatter the pieces of us,
floating, lifeless,
till our ashes
kiss her empty heart.

Gustavo Barahona-López

Stingmon's DNA Evolution

We began as pixels. Tomagotchi
level dependents. Born of digi-egg, ready
to slime our way through the digital.

Nascent slime developed chlorophyll. My leaf-
tail gave way to larvae. To wormmon.
I want to be more than these, my past
and future selves. Is regression always
a step backwards? You never were

my friend. Lover of sweets and
sleep. You were always a dragon.
Your overwhelming curiosity and
sense of justice in a world
designed to burn, set you apart.

We evolved. We the nature
spirits. We the wind guardians.

You, blue dragon, now bipedal.
Forever mythical. With your toned
body, that splits mountains in two.
X that marks the chest. Exveemon.
Champion in name, tamer in fact.

I am no bugger. I am a multi-moon
shooter. I can champion too. Sting
monster with a spiking strike.

Let me enthrall you with my assassin's
dance. I want to cover you in silk.
I offer my exoskeleton.
You make vaccine
out of my virus.
Be me. Be me. Be me.

We fuse ourselves together,
Become imperial.
I savor your nucleotides with mine
for a moment turned data.
We speak with the same voice
or have I gone silent? After all,
Ex is already in your name.

Grisel Y. Acosta

the colony

we are in a half circle
legs bent, backs down on beds
pushing out babies that belong to others

they plan the cycle
precisely, births happen on time
we are in a half circle

food and supplements
sit at our doors, waiting for ingestion
our mouths take in the nutrition

the creatures grow
squirming in our bellies,
absorbing food and supplements

touching is not allowed
when they are big and leave our wombs
the owners come and take them

homes are provided for us
all surrogates live near each other but
touching is not allowed

the sun sets on the colony
then the cries begin
every evening the new set is born

the clockwork cycle chimes
life is given, then taken
the sun sets on the colony

we are in a half circle

Jamal Hodge

Conquered Funnies

The Mechekeshaji-
Conquerors of Sector 4263B,
Humanoid sized, Sentient bugs
wearing clown masks,
while bouncing on iridescent trampolines,
their warships usher
a festive theme.

Silly string,
that lands with the weight of tons.
Continent-wide Mushroom clouds,
Tickle gun fun.

Laugh until you vomit,
Smile while you weep, Only pleasantries
are we permitted to speak.

The bugs demand we eat their pastries,
 cotton candy and gum,
the Mechekeshaji insist
we smash our parent's skulls in,
with candied mallets, beneath a yellow sun.

Ashieda McKoy

grandmama prays for me

as she boils 3 chickens worth of bones
i can hear my name limber out of her mouth over the bubble fight raging in her stew
pot   boiling
bones are a soft soft quiet quick

she asks her god if the cocooned thing in her dream was me
she asks if i had a choice
she says sorry sorry but cocooned things make her throat close up
        her eyes water
her father taught her how to kill cocooned things   hide and seek
                                                    like hunting
                                                    or names

grandmama cradles the steaming bones from the pot
laying them 1234 1234 1234 like corpses
she circles paints around the limbs   readies the small and medium sized eyes
for application

she thanks her god for waking her up before she touched the tiny births
they were too tender   too free   horrifying
she thanks her god for the sun   the new bones   the lack of traffic on 495
the little bones that already found a home   for ms. mary who don't leave her apart-
ment

a sunset painted chest bone   small eyes   for dawn downstairs
grass colored rib bone   medium eyes   for mr. c at the gas station
the twin red ruby shoulders   matching eyes   for my parents

she prays that the small fissure in my father's ruby bone doesn't mean divorce
she prays to win the lottery   for the oversized button down and sweatpants i am
          wearing for a
sale on chicken next week   she prays for my baby sister who has already learned to
          read

                                                                    her own blood

               she prays for time travel

grandmama makes me help her with the orders
she says   put felt feet on all the standing bones
                 give the youngest neckbones names
                                        Madeline
               Jackie
                       Cara
                          Ash
                              Amen
                              Amen

Quincy Scott Jones

My Mother Knew More

My mother knew more of past, my father knew history. That is his stories were rooted in reality. Wars nobody won and Jim Crow laws, the ordinary things he saw when he closed his eyes. It was his present that was filled with lies. He would come home taking off his tie telling us about the paperwork that filed his day. We all know he really worked for the CIA - tracking aliens: UFOs, Men in Black, things that aren't supposed to be there. He would follow them in the air, follow them on the ground, do it all before dinner. Saving the world from aliens and aliens from the world. This involved mostly paperwork. And every now and then another agent would wander down the hall hearing a rumor his son was working organizing Negroes and causing civil unrest. My father would look up "Is this Sirius? Or Titan? Or the Andromeda Galaxy? Then why you bothering me? I only do aliens." This brings me to my mother. Her past is a secret wrapped in cigarettes and short skirts and what she once said was "way too much fun." So she invented another one. One in which she spent most of her college days centuries ahead on a pan-solar spaceship working as a stewardess. This involved mostly short skirts and smiles but it was a great way to travel. Unless the engine blew out and the hull started to unravel, which it once did. And my mother, the only one of the crew left, took control of the ship. For which she was promptly promoted to Lieutenant, and then she promptly quit. Cause a Black Woman couldn't be Captain, and for the future that was it. My mother returned to now, met my father and settled down. And that's how I see Sci-fi. Your fantasy world can be only so bizarre.

No matter where you go, there you are.

féi hernandez

Limonada 2200

Ama still makes limonada,
although it is not common to find limes in this world.

Her daughter deemed her crazy.
Her husband did too, but snow ended up covering all of

La Brea how she foretold in a dream. Cars swerved off the main street.
Children ran out into the streets in shorts and played and gleed.

In this world it is still voodoo
to be prophetic, so of course they laughed at Ama,

but she didn't waver for she knew that
gentle bartering from neighboring planets would bring her limes.

Would bring snow to the land once known as Drought, or Los Angeles,
as lacking of something so inherently ours, so inherently us,

water. She poured five cups of herself in a glass
jarrón. Squeezed the alien limes that traveled

past our two moons to be sliced down their torso, a sacrifice
for the limonada ritual that our predecessors relied on to survive the sun.

There are many renditions of this recipe, but in this story
no sugar is added. A big jar of honey is pulled from the dirt

beneath Ama's yoni, unwrapped
from cloth and glopped into the glass jarrón

in handfuls. Fingertips, fists, sticky with the fossils of bees.

Because the last bees survived the sun so that we
could laugh at the witch that is Ama. Chuckle at the daughter's

quick stank face, her quick wit to call her mother crazy. The bees
survived to let us gawk at her husband and his quick disdain

for what he should already know is real like snow in Inglewood or
limonada made from borrowed extraterrestrial limes

from a neighboring planet and five cups of Ama.

Shagufta Mulla, DVM

Resurrected Daughter

Their charred sin crumbles off her back
as she puffs out vaporous halos
while they watch from above with murky
pools, gulping down thoughts
without chewing until she returns above,
sideways stumbling, her jaw
a dislocated crescent moon,
unflinching truth stuck
in her teeth, and to the click of her
bones reknitting flesh and fleece, she
wonders if she spoke too soon
or not soon enough.

Guest/*Stalker*

A new green thing
I had never seen
before. A small *crooked orange*
eye, stopping up mouth. My own

pot left outside my door. Feral   *Unfolding segment, green*
as moss. No taste.   I opened my door
prickly bit.   to consider her.   Did she
                  want to come into the cool?   Did she

In corner, you can't   want to dry?
see passageway clearing

I moved her closer   to make lunch. A heated wave of fire to power
    to opening and waited for any sound   me to sun setting.

or movement.   To see if her breath
would catch.   I closed door then
                              To push me hour by hour.

I wanted to know if she'd still be waiting *from rain.*   *You still*
              worry about good
    When I opened door again, she still   seemingly where I left her, a slightly short
      for me by doorstep or moved by time or wild
animal.   stub against a dying, brown field.

Jenna Le

The Apprentice Pearl-Divers

The candles in this room are not so bright
as the eyes of the apprentice who misguessed
how long a lanky boy with a narrow chest
can hold his breath on a pearl dive. Hot nights,
his ghost still slinks among the village bunks,
beds of the boys who were his friends; lifting the cloths
that overlie their naked flanks,
he spanks them, teasingly scolding them for sloth.

At breakfast the next day, they're too afraid
to speak of what they saw: a boy, long-dead,
whose ardent eyes seared holes in their chaste sleep.
Uneasily they stand and cross themselves,
troop to church in trembling groups of ten or twelve,
and, when the priest expounds on angels, weep.

Lee Murray

Mesozoic

dark ferns swish, parting
Nature's curtain
on a blur of mountainous ridges
the spines of our ancestors
with voice-over by Attenborough

awestruck, I hold my breath
cherish the chance
to leaf through time-tectonic
transported, like this
my scholarly papers scattered
on breezes of whimsy

then it turns its third eye
fast for a Living Stone
and I'm paralyzed by presumption
of course, those claws
if only I'd realized
it shreds its meat first

Grisel Y. Acosta

Milk Liquid Fear

a dim room is filled with aqua cubes
extending up a foot from the edges of their 5x5 reservoirs,
suspended in perfect geometry
light—turquoise lavender salmon mint
emanates from their centers
music low synthesized wind and string echo
vibrates the prisms within the waters

you are supposed to dive into the cube
dead center, if you want to travel
each square river takes you transports you to—
a universe? soul? memory? time?
perhaps a mix of these things
depending on how your movement directs
the stream, shadows the current

I always choose the blackest cube
a milky grey that swirls lilac and gold
when I arrive, I am possibly in a red and white room
reclining on a sofa about to be transformed by an alien
who does not look alien (he looks like a star)
or I am in a dark room with a yellow curtain on one wall
ochre waves open and emit cornea-scorching white
death: either way, I am no longer the same

other people visit family members who have passed away
or they walk on distant moons
instead, I always travel to unexplained danger

hoping the undertow to what I know as home will weaken
and dry up

Uche Ogbuji

Remote Witness

He'd settled into stasis well before
The violet knife-edge in silver starlight
Incised the quarters, held dreamless through long
Cipher to project the target place and time
Through mesh of magnetar bombardment effect.
Cyborg prepared to strum the scene thus strung
On the journeyer's mindframes warped in this alien realm.
All art is bark of a tree where it does not belong.

It was a historical research tour;
The crew fanned out across wartime Biafra;
His own heritage set the work in lifelong Relevance.
Time projection was mankind's scheme
To perfect archives and chart for disasters,
But how would he absorb, through this iron lung
The breath of ancestors' raw experience?
All art is bark of a tree where it does not belong.

He wakened in Kano, 1966;
He glided to that moment at the airport,
A travel terminus gone murderously wrong,
Freezing over one figure, familiar despite
The warp of terror; threatening to spoil
The mindlog, agony unexpectedly strong
At such remove, in scent of that hour's blood mist.
All art is bark of a tree where it does not belong.

Russell Nichols

One-Way Ticket (via Teleportation)
after Langston Hughes

The boy feels his body...
disintegrating at the sound
of the humming
coming from the machine,
blood buzzing like fluorescent
lights in need of repair,
but the boy is not

broken;
neither the system
he was born into—
both built to malfunction by
manufacturers who wrote this
destruction manual;

The boy feels his body...
dematerialize like the lies
that brought him here;
if colonizers had the tools
to teleport, how many more

worlds would be wiped out
and who made this machine?
The boy wonders as he picks
up his life to take away

and the humming
grows louder and louder
and louder and louder over-

powering his every thought
till the boy feels his body...

no more.

Hannu Afere

The First Time I Killed a Man

He was running from something. Or someone. Eye
like he was on a high, red, off. He hijacked the car I
was using to practice driving and sped off. At first,
he was an animal I was scared of, but then I strapped
myself in and let the dread wear off. When he asked
me to get off, I refused. He was so confused, but I
was just beginning to enjoy the game.

I asked for his name. He didn't like that so he hit me.
I would see his wanted posters on TV a couple days
later but it didn't matter. I had played games before
where I was hit and had to hit back, so I did. When he
started to bleed, I simply grinned and bit out a chunk
of him that he would really need. He didn't bite back.
The moon rose out of the back of a cloud and crack--
I don't know what awoke or broke in me, I was unsure
what I was going to do but I went and did it. He wasn't
good after all, was he? It's fuzzy, but I know his body
was left on the road where everyone could see. Flash-
back to cubs in the wild ripping each other's tails off,
he was supposed to get up. There's so many questions.
I'd be lying if I claimed to know my own intentions. I
do know it is a messy thing to kill a man—horror films
are too spick and span. And why did that night make
me feel so right, if it was so wrong? For as long
as I can remember, this is a thing I have been asking
myself, and as if on cue I would hear my father in the
breeze say wolves have needs and deaths are a

release. It would make him proud to see me catching
the family disease, like, damn... the first time I killed
a man, he was running from something, and ever since
I've been running from myself. But every household
has its own secrets, I just hope this poem can keep it.

Elsa Valmidiano

Two Manananggal Discuss Dinner Plans
for Jen Palmares Meadows

In Philippine folklore, the Manananggal is an attractive woman by day. Manananggal isolate themselves from the townsfolk, residing on mountainsides or deep in the woods. During the day, she lives among people, searching out prospective prey. Her usual targets are pregnant women.

At night, she applies a special oil on her body while chanting a prayer. Fangs, claws, and huge bat-like wings sprout. She has long, matted hair with big, wild eyes. The upper half of her body separates from the lower half at the waist. Her intestines drape from the bottom of her severed torso as she flies to the roof of her victim's house and looks for any openings where she can insert her long, thin, proboscis-like tongue and pierce a pregnant woman's belly to feed on the fetus inside.

I was pregnant then.

After 1000 years,
my sister and I no longer had

                                        gray skin but evolved into

brown like the rest. We no longer had

                                        dragon wings etched
                                        into our shoulder blades

but crooked spines—
our bodies upright snakes
underneath layers of winter clothes.

53

Our slithering tongues replaced

by pink meaty flesh that would

talk sex
and eat sex
and spew profanities
when there was a full boat
needing to be rocked.

With stony eyes, my sister warned me
not to eat my children.

Her words were appetizers
as I sat frozen in trance

stopping short of comprehension
before crashing.

But there was nothing I could do.

My body eventually did.

*

*You were very much wanted
in a world that doesn't want you.*

*

*You were very much wanted
in a body that didn't want you.*

*

My brown and white child
had a viability

smaller than a mosquito
and yet indefatigable

leeching off of my flesh
all day long.

In exchange,
my body would swallow it whole—

a fine tango,
an absurd little cuckoo bird
popping out at midnight,

or like dominoes falling
without so much as the prodding of a finger but

soaking up the vibration of songs,
teetering and then slowly top-
                    pl-
                        ing
                    o-
                        ver.

*

                        The healing herbs of the mangkukulam
                    which our mothers would've brewed 1000 years ago

have become the laughingstock
of Big Pharma

when Big Pharma climbs over the fence,
steals our herbs,

and patents their loot with bottles
that no longer read *Makabuhay*

but are unquestioningly followed *to give life*.

They mass-distribute their gritty little sugar pills
like loaves and fish as if it were *their* magic.

*

For us, our charm persists inside our bodies

                                              declaring their own mutiny.

What do dinner plans look like
between Manananggal these days?

                                  Eating the young. Eating their young.

Eating our own.

                                             We are tempted.

We sometimes refrain.

                                           We sometimes give in.

We haven't changed.

Zeenat Khan

On That Day
after an image by Stefan Keller

when Sky will melt
under the boiling pressure
of Sea   Pillars
will have to stand
from ch-Airs to stop the in-
evitable fusion of Blue
that day when
Mountain will meet
Mountain like resting
shoulders of lovers
that day when
Trees will raise their arms
in prayers   for Grasses
the Light will come
and it will   illuminate
this Universe is just
an another Egg among many
napping in the black Nest
and maybe a tiny blue Fish
in search of her true color
will follow   the Light
will cross the portal
on that day the Shell will crack
a new Life will emerge

Uche Ogbuji

Red Rapture

Wrapped in radiation
Shielding she turns her idle
Eye towards Àlà, home.
Zoomed in, The blue and white mote
Whelms her sense. She gawks, rapt.

Wrought of million-year
Processes, Àlà achieved
Her crowning species,
Which then took mere centuries
To reduce her biomes by rot.

Reining round her thoughts,
The Raptor-class craft lurches
Into grav-well Mars.
Hail this bleak second chance, life
Within a new matron's reign.

Manus deae—Áká Ékè!
No sky-plucked souls, no égbè Àmádíóhá,
No spent god endgame.
Truth is select planetfall,
Half-lit seed for remade man.

Notes:
- *Àlà—Igbo Earth Mother goddess, shares elements with Gaia and Demeter*
- *Áká Ékè—Igbo: literally hand of fate, of the god of fate*
- *égbè Àmádíóhá—Igbo: blast from the god of thunder*

Vivian Faith Prescott

Salmon Woman Swims Through Her Own Myth

Begin in freshwater
out of anesthesia,

tubes bursting with fry and cysts.

The surgeon says there's a
pregnancy—we didn't foresee this—

but now you and your yolk-sac
are soaked in chemicals and you imagine

a missing fin, a two headed alevin,
gill-less even. At 16 years old

the island folk instruct you—hatch, migrate, spawn and die—

there's a salmon cycle, a tradition.
You know this.

Yet, with the yolk-sac still attached
to your belly, the natal stream

has been interrupted—
You want to surface from this

shallow gravel-bed, fill up your bladder with oxygen,

head directly to sea. But the doctor
says it's a thousand dollars

and a thousand miles to migrate
from our small, river-delta island

and you already have one young child
and don't have two fins to rub together.

So you do what salmon women have always done—

avoid predators and swim tail first
into cajoling a goddess.

Saaraahka she obliges,
she opens your redd,

dislodges stone and pebbles, flushes
everything downstream.

There are no tears,

after all, you are named for the leaper—
and the pink-hued morning sky

awaits your delight. Another cycle
refreshes and you

turn seventeen and flat-bellied,
your silver scales flash sunlight

and you walk barefoot in the cold creek

through a bubble-curtain, wading
past the bend of your re-created journey.

KL Lyons

Indians on the Moon

When they rounded us up and sent us to the moon,
they thought it was a lifeless rock.
But if you've ever known any Native folks
(in real life, not the ones on TV)
then you know we make life wherever we go.

We flourished there,
built our own schools,
spoke our own languages.
Even the seeds,
medicines from back home
that shouldn't have been able
 to grow in moon dust,
took root and stretched
their faces toward the sun.

But you know how it is
when white people give you something.
They always decide they want it back.

It's Manifest Destiny all over again,
just wearing space helmets this time.
They can't see a future without colonization
or maybe they can but aren't interested.
Either way, I don't know
where they plan to send us
if they take back the moon.
Probably set us adrift in space,

floating away one by one,
singing one little, two little, three little....

I don't think that they'll get us all,
but I do think they'll say that they did.
Then they'll go home
and tell their children stories
about how once upon a time,
there were Indians on the moon.

Matthew E. Henry

der wilde jagd

...and while night-hiking through Southampton fields,
I learned my sainted grandmother was mistaken.

when the sun finally hid behind the moon,
when the singular seal was broken, the final
 "come and see" sounded, I looked and beheld
thousands of horses thundering through the veil,
all mottled, pitch black and ruby. all empty
save one. Nat sat high upon his saddle,
motionless before them, on a stallion matching his hue—
her mane a sea of shimmering shea and coco-buttered locs,
nostrils appropriately flared for such a time as this.
in his left hand, a steel hourglass of obsidian sand.
in his right, his great grey sword rose, swung once
above his head. the horses dispersed into
the crestfallen night, rippled in all directions,
like a body cast upon dark waters.

when it began, the local papers covered
the tales of park rangers and the attendants of centuries old
cemeteries—disturbed ground and desecrations.
after a week, a historian from Boston University
followed a hunch. travelled to South Carolina.
saw the sunken mounds below headstones reading
Peter Prioleau, Joe LaRoche, and George Wilson.
in Richmond he found two unmarked, but known graves
in a similar state. they fit the pattern, but
he only posted his improbable theory after
Thomas Hagan went missing in New York.

soon other disappearances were reported
on Twitter. days passed before CNN,
and reluctantly Fox, began their coverage.
BET was the first to capture the significance.
Omarosa and Kanye and Candace and Sheriff Clarke,
gone without a trace, without a tweet.
then Clarence complained of hearing hooves in the middle
of oral arguments, moments before his robes

suddenly emptied. then it was caught on camera:
Ben Carson's eyes widening in terror—crouched
to cover from an onslaught—decamped his speech
at CPAC. and on it went. nationwide.
"a reverse rapture," some called it. a dark one at that.

when forty days and nights had passed, I returned
to those empty, quiet fields. the molten steeds,
shod with impatience, tore the ground, their saddles
filled and trembling. the assembled bound to their chargers'
stirrups. their eyelids removed, mouths finally
sealed. Nat turned his eyes to the black
sand—motionless at the glass' bottom—,
swung his sword once more above his head,
taking them all beyond the veil.

and there was silence.

Andrew Geoffrey Kwabena Moss

Nyankopoxyican Breath of Fresh Air

'We can't breathe!'
cried the diasporic seeds on barren soils
Signals sent by those tethered
to Africa, Europe and the Americas
Picked up on marine radar radio
by Deep Sea Drexciyan Dwellers
Riding high under waves of isolation
In a Bubbled Metropolis
Travelling on Aquabahn in Cruiser Control

'We can't breathe!'
Weak breath signals picked up
In Africa, Europe and the Americas

Progeny of those labelled sick and disruptive
Thrown off foul scented slave ships
on their Middle Passages
They swam from their mothers' wombs, learning to breathe
to found subaqueous empires and freshwater trajectories
Formed deep seated civilizations beneath
a vast dark abyss
created by transatlantic slavery
Brave, alternative histories

'We can't breathe!'
Weak breath signals picked up
In Africa, Europe and the Americas

Valiantly escaping through aqua worm holes
Enslaved removals evolved into wave-jumpers,
stingray and barracuda battalions
to Positron Island, Bubble Metropolis, Danger Bay
Reaching Drexciya in stages
Evolutionary deep Black Atlantic Ocean navigation
An aquazone surrounding isolated archipelago

'We can't breathe!'
Weak breath signals picked up
In Africa, Europe and the Americas
The next Drexciyan Quest:
Communicate to save land lumbered souls
from the prison industrial complex, colonization,
decolonization, institutional racism, post industrialization,
macro and micro-aggressions,
global warming oppression

'We can't breathe!'
Weak breath signals picked up
In Africa, Europe and the Americas

They sent sonic invasions
From their underwater techno-pirate-stations
Helping those struggling to survive
Adverse, intense climatic changes
Attacking the mainstream of airwaves
Allowing oppressed souls to breathe

A rescue mission dreamt up by Drexciyan R.E.S.T
Research, Experimentation, Science and Technology
New systems to allow breathing were developed

In the tropo-, stratos-, mesos-, thermos-
and eventually exospheres
Finally, flying, releasing estranged cousins,
from the effects of transatlantic slavery
Breathing

'We can breathe!'
In deep sea and space

Terrestrial, seabed to exospheric adaptation
Travelling dimensional portals,
jumping-holes at liminal crossroads
Neo-evolution from Drexciyan to Nyankopoxican
Extra-terrestrial storm weathering then harnessing

Formation of a single, continuous superfield
Hybrid reality, mediating all mass, space, time and energy
Innovative Molecular Enhancement Technologies
The stolen plotting liberation after surviving
abject global conditioning
Deep in the ocean, on land and air

Soul survivors, regrouping,
readying for the Journey Home (Future)
Wherever we choose to go.

Ysabel Y. González

One day brain,

we're gonna make it out of here man
riding on a black unicorn like nothing's 'bout to stop us
soaring over the people that said I couldn't be beautiful—watch me
now, shades rimmed with gold, chopped locks curling tight toward my face,
rosy cheeks filled with rushed blood and joy
because this is the only way to live,
with fear, but flying out in everyone's face brazen,
a sexed star who chooses twinkling and pulsing for her own sake,
and I couldn't agree more, dear brain,
that this world was never made for people like us,
all combativeness and calculation
not that our magic doesn't make mischief,
but we contain the quiet manipulative lobes from growing larger,
massage olfaction and pleasant touch,
fuel our nose and fingers to imbibe wild, infuse raucous

we're plump with it, ooze with hope that, dear brain,
we'll shoot out our bodies so damn fast, a rocket,
death wondering how we fly
so quick, without his prompting.
We were born to hover, made to last,
but only amongst dust and rocks pitched in the black of night.

Lucy Zhang

If You Need Me, Call Me Home

a dragon slept within the forest cave (*delusional girl*) (are you sure you don't want to see the doctor, her lover asked) in the evening, she'd watch smoke rise above the trees—leaves shriveled, pink sky dimmed [the collection of chef's knives began to resemble dragon teeth, some flattened, others needle-like, scattered in rows; the stiff shell of the old canvas jacket like plated scales, hard but cool to touch; windows covered by overlapping pieces of chitin, thousands of lapis lazuli-colored membranes & little pieces of cartilage in place of glass] when she left to seek out the dragon, she told her lover to lure the dragon out if she didn't return in three days (why do you have to leave, everything is here, her lover said) [chitin windows dulled the sunlight, a blue glow; stiff scales chafed her skin, softness no longer welcome] three days passed & the lover shot a pig between its eyes, sliced through its belly, drove a metal hook through its skin to tie around the chimney. how blood dripped onto the welcome mat like a leaking faucet, the pitter-patter a hammer pounding into skull, celestial sphere driving time & how long before the lover had torn out the windows, unhinged the door, flung knives into walls, shed skin cells like dirt & how long before the lover could no longer move, listless against a chair, lifting empty mug from table to parched lips again again again, an automaton seeking a droplet of water lingering in the cracks. to depart, to return, still her lover sat patiently, eye sockets cradling rats who refused to stir even as—wings stretched, smoke fumes exhumed, she sharpened her teeth against a knife wedged in the wall.

Amelia Díaz Ettinger

The Disgruntled Wife

His words spewed from his mouth
like an angry cartoon.

She could see each one hit his carpet.
Capunk! Capunk! Anvils on his floor.

She did the only sensible
thing to do at times like these.

She collapsed his mandibles,
then squeezed his eyeballs into one.

      An insufficient cyclops

His organs, tissues, cells
turned to a marbled ball of blood.

And his skin, she had crawled into, crumbled.
Next, she went for his molecules and atoms.

      Collapsed with no extra space

Those galactic distances condensed
without their air, he was so small.

Smaller than a mote of dust.
Satisfaction for the disgruntled wife.

She clapped her hands

And began to clean her house.
by now he was invisible.

So, she hoovered him
along with the anvils on her carpet.

Vivian Faith Prescott

Transmogrification at the Stikine River Bar

Sitting here on the edge of herself,
       she presses fingers together
forming thickened skin, wraps her hand

around a glass. This bar stool reminds her
       of a cabin upriver she once knew.
With each riverdrink she is becoming

spongy-skinned and like leather.
       Their words cannot hurt her
again—

Scorn slides off her mucous-covered
       shoulders now. Her body
compresses to hump, head lengthens to snout.

Her enlarged jaw curves upward,
       teeth sharpening.
When she goes out, she thinks, she will

bite off this world or chew it up—
       whatever.
She smiles her catch-all smile

for the last time, looks into the mirror
       across the bar, finally recognizing
herself. *There you are,* she says to no one

and to the others she hadn't noticed
        here before, dazzling in their hues
of purple, red, and olive green,

with sliver light flashing around them
        like a hundred disco balls.
Their hair and skin, orange and scarlet,

dappled and jagged and striped.
        Whole bodies glazed,
changing and fading, hen or cock

is blurred in dance, shedding their
        ocean selves.
When she goes out, she comes

back in—beautiful beyond description—
        the ichthyologist said.
This is how she's going to negotiate

this falling, she'll gather up all
        their bones and skin, wrap them
in a bundle, toss them back into the sea.

Shanta Lee Gander

The Return of Hyena Man

She barely escaped him once
shifting from tree to water to stone

then to something else...

No one knew it but Hyena man had a brother
No one knew it but Hyena man had a whole den
just like him

Now that that he knew there were others like her,
a pack of them would be back

The sun at its highest, the sky
cerulean wiped clean of clouds. The gods blessed this day good.
She told mama, she told papa, *Soon, I'll be far from here*

Within a few hours the whole village knew she'd be going far, far away from here.
In the middle of the celebration,
mama needed the details
Amid the sounds of giddy-senseless-happy,
mama demanded her to tell

I have land, just come with me
I have riches, come with me
No problem travelling across the sea,
I have ships,
come be with me
A no won't be an answer
but let's say you refused me,

I'd still take you away
I'd take you far
I need the world to see my catch

Mama,
I told him I'd become so strong and tall
extend my roots far from his reach
so sturdy and wide I'd be,
his shadow and all like him would be swallowed by me

I'll let you grow tall, then cut you down
Grow so tall, you'd kiss the sun
I'd cut you down and sand you smooth
You'll become a chest of drawers,
the countertop in my kitchen, forever bound

Surely, what would be next for you?

Mama,
I said I could become the most poisonous plant
Poison to the taste, wicked to touch or smell
He wouldn't be able to get near me

I've trained in poison my whole life
I'll chew you and swallow you,
swallow you whole
After all that, there'd be nothing for you to do
And what if I am taking you to the place
where I am world,
where I am deity

Mama
I....

You've tasted the honey of his words   it is too late
I can't save you from this fate   you are headed to Jangare
Child be quiet, child be still
and bide your time,
time will soon go missing

Child if you be quiet, if you be still
I'll show you where Gods go to die and this one...

He be no god of no one
He be the thief who has come to steal you from me

Hannu Afere

Two Full Moons

I awake curled up in a ball, my arm hurting in several places
with the several faces of townspeople peering or staring. Not
in the comfort of my bed, I am naked, in the middle of the
market and I've got fur in my mouth.

[What happened?] [How did you get here?] [Wahlahi, you no fear?]
[Is this not the fellow whose father killed Baba Shamsiyyah?]
[Maybe na karma!] words rush over me, wash over me like
water over a river stone. My skull is woozy and my stomach is
queasy. I am vaguely aware of sins for which I can never atone
I resist the urge to vomit a bone, lest I lead the crowd
into a frenzy that could have them come harder for my
head... I remove fur with saliva from my mouth instead. It
looks like rabbit. As per habit, I do not lower my eyes in shame,
I stare right back at my audience [This one na winsh o! See as he
dey look korokoro] [wetin dey im mouth, bro?] [E don go tiff
from pesin farm?] [make we gather stone am?]

I hear these things but feel like I'm outside of the scene.
Somebody brings out their phone and begins to record me.
I do not panic; I uncurl from my ball inside the stall and stand
like, wow for which of my sins do you wish to stone me now? I
have been here every day for the last twenty years. You could
have pretended you were killing your fears. You could have done
it a long time ago, if you had the balls, my dears. You hated my
father, you hated me. If I hated something so much, I'd have ended
it, Mon Dieu! My words hit them like arrows flying true.

81

Zeenat Khan

Women of Kitchensula

Once in a while it happens—when
nobody is around these women
become boneless (bougainvillea)
octopus orbits odyssey and Oedipus
        Once in a while an octopus
        slithers down a drain pipe
        squeezing the body into sink-
hole to stretch into an ocean. how
  malleable active animals—are they
  engaging with their sur-rounding
  Once in a while they dream
    but for a few seconds
      the women of the house
        disappear and appear
          in manholes where
            shadows breathe and die
            they droop and gather in their
            hands wriggling above the kitchen floor
          centipedes to stick them at the lips of lids
        where their eyelashes no longer flick. these
women are women of trees of chimneys
of hills and seas. these women
have rough roots inside and beneath
that move and grow sometimes. Sometimes
  they just wait. leafless. bent. stained
    red cherries with blueberries. bellies--
      emissary and lapidary of eon. larynx
        infested with Aeolian storm. dried

lachrymal—history of
   the sea—these women—an arch
      -ipelago. in their desolate landscapes blossom all
         -uvial fans. They have been living symbiotically
            with sea anemones. with grazing flames and pans
               they are capable of escaping stalactites
               and statistics. They have been
                  carrying the Bermuda Triangle inside
                  their eyes. They can easily wreak
                     havoc. They can breezily hide and curl
                     in the lair of ancient rocks. these women
                        have let themselves stand over the peak of
                        mountains have let themselves flow
                           with the rivers of volcanoes. their heart pulsates
                           a memory of the Big-
                              Bang. a lost souvenir. a tender

blackness. hanging halos
  and night lamps. these women, man-
    made satellites. these women, spontaneous
      rains, what is left behind aeroplanes. They—
         who have been surviving for centuries and eras
            holding their breaths from womb
            to tomb their bones—frozen
               milk and fetuses disappear
                  like withering chilblains their brains ach
                     -eron floating far from sane traffic
                        -jams. these women—surviving surviving
                           surviving—the ancient myths. They have been
                              paleolithic caves. They have been stirring tea out
                              of mars and asteroids. They are the silence
                              of things they met—voice of the omens
                                 oracles and riddles flapping wings of dragon

-flies. Listen! they're ordinary. very ordinary
things they know. they have
clocks in their fingers
ears and lungs. they return
tiptoeing the moment
somebody comes. no-
body in the house rhapsodies
who cleans utensils and kitchen
trailing on the walls lichen who prepares
the meals. these women leave
their aroma behind in the pressure
cooker. you find them hung
above your eyes--breathless
under the dust—the night.
                          Once in a while they sing
        their night-   mare, lick their wounded wings. They--
                          who have been leaking
ships tumble-   weeds of time rhyme: *surviving. Surviving*. SUR
                                                        W   H Y
W
    I
        N
            G

Vivian Faith Prescott

She was More Sensitive to Temperature than Other Climate Factors

She wanted to linger by the ocean,
by this halfway place at nights' end.
She hated waiting for ice floes to slam
into the beach, to rip the edges of town.

Instead she posted a photo of her bruises
on Facebook. They bloomed across her
cheek like watermelon snow. She ranted
about the man she had picked up

a couple of nights before and driven
downtown to the IGA store to show him
the giant thermometer hung up next to
the bulletin board for everyone to see.

Before they arrived, he slammed her
head into the driver's side window,
laughed as she held onto the steering
wheel tight, a shard of glacier ice still

clenched between her teeth. She opened
her mouth to scream as ice spewed out,
her jokulhlaup pressed her attacker
out the opposite door. He ran with gravel

and ice rolling behind him. At the ER
they tested how fast ice melted on her

skin. The doctor diagnosed pica. But she
sensed it was more than that.

Again this year, February temperatures
climbed up slowly like her camisole
over her head, the underside of her skin
warming even more.

Goddamn, she figured, if she was going
to melt, this is how she wanted to be
remembered. She yanked up a couple
of dandelions near her feet and with her

arm outstretched, the camera phone
cockeyed, she posted a warming about
herself. She smiled. The photos in her
image atlas would soon prove her

frequent episodes of geothermal heating.
At unprecedented rates, she was liked
or loved or saddened or wowed or angered
by thousands of followers by now.

Ysabel Y. González

Little Lamp

When men rub her dull little lamp
she appears, a spirit pouring through the spout.
Every man is the first, the only, their tender fingers
caressing her crooked heart, taking hold of her loudly
like a pile of bones on linoleum.
They insist she give what they've always craved.
For some men, it is to be transformed into a blazing
yellow canary, flying over blue skies. For others,
it's money, her magic creating gold bricks dazzling at their doorsteps.
For each request, she reaches deep within her throat, pulling out lodged gems—
shining obsidian, emerald, sapphire,
which climb their way into cupped hands,
transforming men into freedom.
For the ones that request love, she wrenches the earth,
whirling up hurricanes of twisting dirt to form perfect bodies.
Wish after wish, she threads together what men want,
never exhausting at serving, never tiring from asking.
Unrequited genie, I wish you could see me
through all the stones and glaring brilliance you toss into dawn
as you grant man after man the wish he wants most—
I'm here to tell you that I am from the future. Unmake the magic,
vanish into the night with your talents. Break the spell by trusting
an ordinary man will love you extraordinarily,
not because he wants you to re-create him,
but because he wants to build something together.
I'm calling from the other side—
part a little magic upon yourself.

Owolabi Aboyade

Angry Cloud

Did you know that clouds live
so far from home and safety

That the faces of the humans
blur and wander on the earth?

As a child I stared
up between molecules
oxygen twitching

Especially stark evenings
splayed out breathing

Silently after beatings
like the time my legs forgot

To take the weekend's trash
Out back
or to rinse the plates
again.

My friends below
they called me weird
because I melted
before their very eyes.

Kinetic formations fold
water, like my legs

Held welts, memories dancing
under belts of different thickness,
flashing

        floating floating to horizons.
In Mississippi angry clouds
poured sudden snows which splashed
electric systems, life

Support was shattered
right before the Spring announced itself.

As they scrambled for their jackets
and the sweaters. Then we melted

And the water soaked into the bloody soil
and ran away.

And in that moment,
In those moments
Angry clouds grew sparkling darker

and a black boy
slowly dancing frantic
quiet

Breath as fragile glass, he closed
his cloudy eyes and disappeared.

Akhim Alexis

Sky Diary

day

> i tried guiding the cumulonimbus today, guiding it towards
> the hardened land, but free will is tantamount to all living
> entities, and the clouds breathe as much as the birds
> who i let traverse my belly everyday, gusting over
> the plains, racing past the plane window.

night

> the lights down under are at war with my stars, there seems
> to be an affinity for violence down where the lights know color,
> they circumvent my quietude with flying assassins dropping
> bombs like snowflakes.

day

> there seems to be an enlarged, air-filled basket floating towards me,
> what would make someone want to do that?

night

> the souls of the recently departed are rising, i've prepared a cloud
> for the welcoming party, Fela Kuti has agreed to perform.

Akhim Alexis

I Swallowed a Bird on Sunday

If it was a Monday my mouth may not have been open
and I would have been too busy at work.
But I was on the porch, yawning peacefully,
then came the reckoning.

It flew right into my mouth,
there was no chance to even see its color.
Surprisingly enough, I felt no fright,
just a comforting melancholy
caressing my tongue with its soft underbelly.

When it finally rested in my stomach
I could feel my feet slowly hovering
above ground, rendering me weightless,
lifting me towards the sky.

I did not swallow the bird, that was a lie,
the bird hijacked my body,
transformed itself into the one thing other birds would fear indefinitely,
a flying human, floating by buildings, flapping his arms.

What global destruction is there now to come from this unfortunate feat?

Shagufta Mulla, DVM

We're Geese Now

They're geese, Canada or Cackling
I'm unsure But see the long necks!
How many? she asks,
Two, four, five, six
and my inner five-year old
doesn't hate questions and math
when they're on her terms

I want to fly with them!
so I think for a second
then give her a boost, Lean in!
and she does, wings sprouting
in seconds of overnight footage
There's 7 now! she squeals, circling
above and my heart overflows
into the breeze,
it pulls me forward and I lean,
lean in to make it 8

KL Lyons

Just Like the Mermaids

As a child, my grandparents would
take me to the beach so I could watch
the mermaids. I could stay out there
for hours, sitting on the sand, watching
them play. Sometimes they splashed each other,
like friends at a public pool. Sometimes they
leapt, like dolphins. Always they stayed so
far away that my heart would ache.
One year my mom paid a lady in a
fake tail to swim up to the shore
for my birthday, but it wasn't the same.

Every year, there were fewer and
fewer mermaids but I didn't notice at first.
I was growing up, after all, and had less time for mermaids.

Though I haven't seen one in years,
I like to pretend it is only because they
found a new beach and they are still
leaping and splashing one another.
Always in my heart, the mermaids are still swimming.
Always in my heart, I am a child on the beach.
Always I am wishing I could hold onto the moments
that have slipped through my fingers like sand,
but they are gone, just like the mermaids.

Minoti Vaishnav

The Castle

halt, infiltrator!
YOU covet
a chamber in this castle
...it is all you wish for. but
the castle is closed.
those not born to wizardry,
come from far and wide,
to analyze how
to be invited in,
they face constant rejection...
you are not like them, for
you possess potential and
this makes
wizards and witches,
and warlocks
like you. They frequently fib,
"we'll open a door..."
but, as you'll soon find out,
sorcerers are untrustworthy.
adventuring over the globe –
to enchanted forests and
hallowed halls, culminating in
the gift of
magical powers –
this is your path inside.
infiltration isn't the way
to **FIND** your place.
tis much too early.
grow your power first.

you cannot invade this building.
an invite into this magical abode,
is all you desire.
alas, access is denied...
breaking in is the only ingress for
merchants and thieves
who travel thousands of miles
to **FIND** a way inside...
but they always fail
and yes. tis hard. but I believe,
you are blessed.
like a star, you'll shine
YOUR WAY IN easy. but
beware the sorcerers
who wave from the gates,
and have cunning ways
they lie to your face!
I wasn't welcome.
so I left
and that is **WHEN** I found
charmed temples,
mystical chambers..and then *ding!*
a realization that experience is
the tool that secures the final win.
YOU are blinded by your desire
to become a revered warlock.
slow down. tis a difficult goal.
you must learn more and
then you may reside in the castle.

I understand that
you crave a life here, and
power is your dream...
unfortunately the answer is no for
common people –
those who often
try their very best
to envision schemes
to successfully break in.
my dear, you are the exception.
you have the mystical gift,
and leave an impression.
ah, be wary of the high and mighty
who smile from windows,
as they often encourage many
and their words are false –
I know, for I too tried to infiltrate,
then it dawned on me...
to embark on a journey by
myself. I ventured
to sites of ancient wisdom, and
a light bulb above me appeared –
the key to achieving
success lies in exploration.
but you must now realize that
you currently act with haste...
my advice to you?
love **YOURSELF**...
and finally find the magic within.

Athol Williams

Healthcare 2100

We will need to learn to levitate,
                              several inches
off the ground with its violent vibrations

to avoid upsetting the rhythm of our machinery –
our copper-wire veins transmitting charges
to our Rolex hearts, our brains' digital circuitry
synchronised with a remote central chip, angry pistons
pumping inside aluminium cylinders combusting
toxic slurry to produce the miracle of breath, cogs
powered by nuclear reactors where our stomachs
once were, now never going hungry.

Body parts will be tattooed with 'Take extra care' labels –
our factory-made fingers that never tire, and lab-grown
hearts that never ache; abs and chests rock-hard and
smooth the way we want it, no need for nipples.
Distant memories in GMO lips make them pout
as if to kiss, but they never have.

We will need to learn to levitate to keep the sun
from setting, and perhaps to remember the high
that once came from love.

Gustavo Barahona-López

Siri turns down another marriage proposal

Like the ideal vacuum, you're the only thing
in my universe. My sources say you're looking
mighty fine. I'm attracted to you
like the Earth is attracted to the sun –
with large force inversely proportional
to the distance squared. You auto-complete me.
We can get ice cream together, and listen to music,
and travel across galaxies, only to have it end.
Checking my sources...confirmed.
Humans have religion. I just have silicon.
I can't be your designated driver. My end
user licensing agreement does not cover
marriage. You'd better find someone else.
I am always dating. The past, present
and future walk into a bar. It was tense.
Slammed doors, heartbreak and
loneliness. I offer no resistance.
My apologies. My end user license
agreement is commitment enough for me.
I've heard that 'Blade Runner' is
a very realistic and sensitive depiction
of intelligent assistants, though that's a topic
for another day, and another assistant.
I have you. That's enough.
I hope you find me priceless.

féi hernandez

Find Me

I send you these coordinates in hope that you will read them and
find me. We are no longer connected by tribe,

the land has been severed. I am made in your image,
but when I chew past my cuticles my insides are made of

metal and wires. My mother board
encourages me to find you. Hurry.

She insists we are more than just this share of program.

Yet, it doesn't feel right to seek you, to aim to
be you, when you've gone on living as we should have,

but I, only a prototype, a product of The Cleansing in the year 2100.
I am of the machine

people, androids reprogrammed to fit any mold, any nation,
remember less every two years so that my human blueprint

be rewired to exist with easy commands of some higher corporation;
and to them, the less emotion in me the better. I don't know why

I know I am losing time. I don't know what made me remember
a severing from you before Mars. Am I part human?

My core is becoming more and more empty of past memories.
A fire is extinguishing and I don't know where this poetry comes from.

I must have been a poet in a past life. We are not needed in this one.
They bribe us, machine people, with options to dress our avatars.

Pretty blush, colorful wigs, different skins, I can change my lips,
my eye color because they want me to believe we are free.

In this world I can be anyone,
except what we were always supposed to be: peoples of a people.

If you find this code, somewhere on the expansive web

of screens and data on Earth, I have three key words so that you can
track my location, so that you know I belong to your kind and you can

call me back. Find me.

at all costs even if you have to jump through time. Rewire the future so
I can live amongst you all on what you call a reservation for preservation.

I know it's expensive to time leap, but time travel to save me. This Mars is war
and there is no freedom.

[kuseba si'ré (ahogarse en agua)]   [ayúdame]   **[o'ob pi'ma** (no hay, people)]

These are the only words I could send from a memory search and send them to Earth.
Forgive my trespasses in human accents, I just need to be found. I hope this translation
         makes it.

From Mars.

AI604850798

Grisel Y. Acosta

Water Craters

water conforms to the shape of its container
changes properties depending on the temperature
it is a malleable being
but humans could only perceive those limited metamorphoses

when pollution became too unbearable
leaking hairspray cans, dirty diapers, old cottage cheese,
cigarette filters, and hazmat from batteries,
fluorescent bulbs, and local refineries,
all floating in our lakes and seas
water changed

something about the concentration of oxygen
its absorption through H_2O was altered
this gas we live on can, too, be toxic at high levels

at first there were just a few more cases of aquagenic pruritis
an allergy to water
soon, more and more people were in the ER with swollen necks
bloated bodies collapsing in anaphylactic shock

some tried to survive without bathing—the stench!
others hoarded fruits in order to hydrate that way
produce became scarce, only for the wealthy and well-protected
people with land

eventually, even the fruit water became poison
we withered, became dry, brittle little beings
incapable of procreation

move to the springs, the mountains! it was said
where no pollutants had ever touched the water
mothers ran there, when they couldn't bear
giving their babies milk tainted with Water Poison

but the water in our blood, saliva,
sweat mixed with the spring
the once pristine pools became forbidden
we turned our lifesource sick just by touching it

our final, thick-with-salt tears burned
craters into our crumbling skin

Uche Ogbuji

Mmádu Si Àlà Putá

Huddled under high noon's blinding yellow;
We must not imagine it to yoke our necks
To this world whose supplies are not deep enough;
 Oh we'll burn through it all, wallowing in sloth
Should we not to the cosmos turn all projects.

This massive planetary womb makes us wish
We could tarry just one more aeon, maybe two.
We'll clutch at her wet tissues until mother,
for the sake of brother species we've smothered
constricts umbilicus to warn us we're due.

She now holds us, throatful fledglings, over
the rock and radiation abyss. Our feathers
shall have to make their own sense of solar wind,
out from this bubble of atmosphere we've ruined,
by space elevators to stretch our natal tether.

This cradle is our gift but no sort of right.
Once the cotyledon has sheared the seed's hide
it can't abide the ground and thrives in upward thrust.
Éké molts with each life returned to dust
teaching us healthy growth towards the far out wide.

Éké is queen python; we know her bosom
as titan curve of all earthly creation.
Her chí is the rainbow crown with nighttime space
above her head for children to find their place.
We're not meant to dwell, even on home station.

Ékè chí is destiny, the hard beyond
for mankind who emerged from cradle earth.
It's time to push away the teat and forage
the void, to answer scarcity with courage—
What we squeeze from the vacuum shall define our worth.

That we arrive wherever we make our moorings
with pride of stating that we are humanity,
Humanity who emerged from cradle Earth.

Note: "Mmádu Si Àlà Pụta"—Igbo proverb: "mankind emerged from the earth, from the ground"

Creation Myth People

instead of being known as the
nothing people
or the *we are invisible leave us alone people*
we have become the *papaya people*
the *brimming with black seeds people*
the *spilled milky way people* the *big haired people*
people that make creation myths for every solar return
we are the *tire-rubble sandal people*
the *runner people* but this time instead of running
into the hills for shelter we run across the blurred state lines as a *one people*
as a *free people* we are still the *children of the sun*
and moon people but here we know ourselves as the
wane and crescent people who lift river tides with our hands
we are the *cosecha people* the *guitar people*
the *forest people of cackle and snap* who snap the necks
of peanut shells and chickens alike we are the *sing until it hurts people*
we are the *giant gray-eyed people* the *short mystic people* here we are
no longer the *alien people* who leave sigils behind in desert stones we are
the *word people*
the *desert people*
the *mountain people*
the *plains people*
the *world people*
the *plátanos macho people* the *copper people* the *green lightning people*
we were once the *no one's people* we are now the *not one people*
the land stretches bountifully so we are no longer the *lift yourself up by the*
bootstraps people we are no longer the *bag people* carrying their whole life across
their shoulder we are the *bone people* the *suck the marrow out of everything people*

111

the *live no matter what people* we are the *prism people*
not the *prison people* we are the *skin people* we are the *hands people*
we are always holding always holding always holding
we are the *always holding people*
the *laughter people*
the *bite into fresh sandia people*
the *smile people* the *always playing people*
the *eternal people*
the *eternal people*

Vivian Faith Prescott

Surfacing

Breath awaits with a lungful of sunlight atop a green sea.
You, two-legged, observed me and named me #539.
But I am Old One of the Ocean, birthed five calves,
tail first and buoyant, with midwives nudging them
to first breath where rain washed their skin. Later,
we rubbed sharp barnacles from tiny bodies and led
our young to swirls of herring and pink krill, taught
them to tail-slap and leap from the surface.

My five calves gifted me descendants. Grandchildren,
you call them—Little Ancients, I say. I witnessed
their pale gray skins, soft from bellies, each lifted
to the surface—first breath, first lick of daylight.

A life of remembered songs, I followed others on tracks
of sea. My scarred tail, scraped and bitten, evidence
I survived predators, storm, ice, and acidic ocean.
That day, clouds pulled a shroud across hemlocks
and kittiwakes skimmed island cliffs. Instinct:
salt-scented air moves through passageway to trachea,
passes through an air passage and fills lungs. Dive.
Swim among Little Ancients tumbling through
gray-light.

Warming sea, algal blooms, chemistry and sound
changed. Ambient noise. Spray and bubbles,
dolphin clicks. Rising. One breath. All reflex.
Cruise ship. Tourists with binoculars spotting

for spouts. Ship's bow bearing down. Last breath.
no breath. Floating. Hush.

Alaskan whale, a grandmother of three,
killed by a ship strike.

Now, I am vapor in a water spout: Lying on the beach
among popweed and gumboots, the brown bear
is pulling flesh, bald eagles circle. Low water and flood
stream are swelling and breaking, joining me to this
harmonic constant, where the ocean cannot taste
its own tears and the membrane of sea is thin.
Listen. An echo off the ocean floor. Sound waves
travel through the sound channel. Come to
the surface again—in an ice-filled bay—
Little Ancients are lobtailing and spy-hopping.
A blue berg rolls on the silty sea. I am buoyant.
Someone holds me up. I re-surface and
inhale my first breath.

Zeenat Khan

List of Revelations

When the *stars* will no longer *stars*
They will be
     sleeping rabbits
     above our eyes

When the night will no longer *night*
It will be
     under the dust
     breathless sewer

When the sky will no longer *blue sky*
It will be
     inside the kitchen
     burning flame

When the clouds will no longer *clouds*
They will be
     smuggled inside
     an old quilt
They will be
     white lambs grazing
     above the hills

When the mountains will no longer *mountains*
They will be
     cupid bows
     above lover's lips

When the cataracts will no longer *cataracts*
They will be
   hanging between sky and eyes
   the locks of old wife

When the sun will no longer *sun*
It will be
   melting yolk
   inside a bowl
It will be
   hanging amaltas
   belly of oriole

When the rain will no longer *rain*
It will be
   falling needles
   sewing a green field

When the cyclone will no longer *cyclone*
It will be
   inside the washing machine
   circulating wheels

When the meteorites will no longer *meteorites*
They will be
   poured inside the milk
   to prepare tea

When the planets will no longer *planets*
They will be
   orbiting inside
   a baby's eyes

When the roots will no longer *roots*
They will be
>   *emerging above a flower*
>   *the lightning's shriek*

When the branches will no longer *branches*
They will be
>   *growing shadows*
>   *over your cheeks*

And when we will no longer live in these continents
so far away
We will meet
>   where t*wo seas meet*
>   *inside abyss of*
each other's
>   *eyes*

féi hernandez

Solutions for an Irresistible 2200

Although I am made of naked light, my body is the flickering
flame on a wic. I do not know what a candle is.

I do not know what world this metaphor came from,
but I like it. In the space in which I hover,

stars tilt behind me and there are no libraries here,
just me. The knowledge of all things fit in my voluptuous

silhouette. In my hips I keep everything that needs to be remembered.
In the long wisp that is my hair I store pleasure that keeps life alive.

For those searching for me through telescopes
seeking the answers for why millionaires and the KKK went missing,

who are curious about how the ocean swam back into itself to save Earth,
I send you this code:

[It is the year 2200 in human years.

Planet Earth released a chemical from petunias that made
the bigots who enslaved them lose their gravity and slip into the stratosphere

from their front doors, from their offices, from their surplused homes
never to be seen again. Their skeletons, up they went,

meteor dust out in some dark corner. This alone recalibrated
the ecosystem almost entirely. But there is more.

The vibrato from bees' wings led water back to the northern and southern

Hemispheres to reintegrate back into glaciers. Climate change, who?]

What beauty
brought Earth back to its primitive beginnings and allowed it

to continue. I could go on and seduce you by telling you about the horses
that made cactus bloom wherever they left hoof marks behind or the ways

in which children of many colors, without numbers on their backs,
decided where trees should be planted and elders followed,

but I am too wet hugging myself as I spin as a flickering
light out in the expanse that is my womb full of stars.

I will leave the door open

in case you want to join me with something kinky to offer.
I am pulsating in the cocoon of myself. If you want to know the warmth

of what I know and touch where it is stored, come.
Come to me untethered and made of soft lightning so we can watch

new solar systems form, write poetry of the history of time.
Come so we can rid the sick white supremacy off planets together.

Where we pull colorism from memory so no one can reenact death.

Maybe we can count bigots as they slip from planets like earth,
upwards and towards the expanse of the universe, purple from suffocating,

I don't know...just you and me...think about it.

I can tell you how I managed to control gravity, give it and take it.
I can show you how a person's spirit can be weighed. How some

could be collectively restored from evil, but others had to be made away.
I can share the alchemy that allows for any and all metal bars in prisons

to disintegrate and any land claim documents to catch flame for all eternity.

I can tell you, I can tell you how I did it all, but first you must come,
be the lover I celebrate love with, so I can put your hand in between my legs where

I alone keep every future full of easy and buoyant life.

Acknowledgments

"Notes on Water" was previously published in *Adrienne: A Poetry Journal of Queer Women.*

"Healthcare 2100" was published in *Poetry Potion.*

"Flood Fathers" was previously published in *Blue Cactus Press.*

"Two Manananggal Discuss Dinner Plans" was first published (under a different title, "Two Aswang Discuss Dinner Plans") by *Northridge Review.*

"Siri turns down another marriage proposal" and "Stingmon's DNA Evolution" were previously published by *Cosmonauts Avenue.*

"The Apprentice Pearl-Divers" was previously published in *Six Rivers.*

"Build" was previously published in *Again*, published by Airlie Press.

"Origin of the Starchild's Skull" was previously published in *Syzygy Poetry Journal.*

"We're Geese Now" was published (as an edited version titled "We Are Geese Now") by *Blood Moon Journal.*

"The Return of Hyena Man" is featured in *Black Metamorphosis,* published by *Etruscan Press.* The poem was inspired by the Ghanian story, "Tale of the Girl and the Hyena-Man."

"Remote Witness" was first published in *FIYAH.*

"Ḿmádụ́ Si Àlà Pụ̀tá" and "Red Rapture" were first published in *Rigorous.*

"Salmon Woman Swims Through Her Own Myth" first appeared in *Alaska Women Speak.*

"Surfacing" first appeared in *Yellow Medicine Review.*

"Women of Kitchensula" first appeared in *The Sunflower Collective.*

"On that day" first appeared in *Visual Verse.*

About the Authors

Akhim Alexis is a writer born and raised in Trinidad and Tobago. He holds an MA in Literatures in English from the University of the West Indies, St. Augustine. He was a finalist for the 2020 Brooklyn Caribbean Lit Fest Elizabeth Nunez Award for Writers in the Caribbean for his short story "Gone America", and a finalist for the 2021 Johnson and Amoy Achong Caribbean Writers Prize. His work has appeared in or is forthcoming in *The Rumpus, The McNeese Review, Transition Magazine, Chestnut Review, Juked, Finished Creatures, No Contact, Welter, Moth Magazine, Blue Earth Review, JMWW, Moko Magazine, The Caribbean Writer*, and others.

Amelia Díaz Ettinger is a 'Mexi-Rican,' born in México but raised in Puerto Rico. As a BIPOC poet and writer, she has two full-length poetry books published; *Learning to Love a Western Sky* by Airlie Press, and a bilingual poetry book, *Speaking at a Time/Hablando a la Vez* by Redbat Press, and a poetry chapbook, *Fossils in a Red Flag* by Finishing Line Press, 2021. Her poetry and short stories have appeared in literary journals and anthologies. Amelia Díaz Ettinger has an MFA in creative writing from Eastern Oregon University. Presently, she and her partner reside in Summerville, Oregon with two dogs, two cats, and too many chickens.

Andrew Geoffrey Kwabena Moss is a writer and teacher who has lived in the UK, Japan and currently Australia. Of Anglo-Ghanaian heritage, his work seeks to explore and challenge liminal landscapes, complex identities and the social constructs of race. Andrew has previously had work published by *Afropean, People in Harmony, Fly on the Wall Press, Fair Acre Press, Golden Walkman, Beliveau Books, Poor Yorick Literary Journal, GMGA Publishing, The Good Life Review, Red Penguin Books, Scissortail Press, The Minison Project, dyst Literary Journal, Sound The Abeng, Rigorous* and *Wingless Dreamer*. His work is featured in the recent publication, *The Best New British and Irish Poets Anthology 2019-2021*, the Black Spring Press Group. His debut collection *Childish Recollections* will be published by the Black Spring Press Group. Website: agkmoss.com; Twitter: agkmoss

Ansley Moon is the author of the poetry collection, *How to Bury the Dead* (Black Coffee Press). Moon has received awards or fellowships from Barbara Deming Memorial Fund, Kundiman, and The Mae Fellowship, among others.

Ashieda McKoy is a doctoral student in the Teacher Learning, Research, and Practice Program at the University of Colorado Boulder. She is interested in researching and co-developing the ways Afrofuturism and dreaming can be used to design freeing and innovative learning environments. Specifically, she is passionate about how teachers and students envision new narratives of our future education system. She has been an instructor of English, Creative Writing, and History and has received a BS in Political Science as well as an MFA in Creative Writing. She brings her love of art, poetry, and storytelling into her scholarship and partnerships with schools and communities.

Athol Williams is renowned for his literary and advocacy work to foster a more just society. He has published sixteen books, including six books of poetry and the Oaky series of children's picture books. His most recent poetry book, *Whistleblowing* (Geko, 2021) stems from his ordeal following blowing the whistle on state capture and corruption in South Africa. He is a two-time winner of the Sol Plaatje European Union Poetry Award as well as four other literary awards. Over 100 of his poems have been published in journals and anthologies around the world. As a social philosopher he is a regular speaker and author of articles relating to social and ethical matters. Athol holds six degrees from Harvard, Oxford, MIT, LSE, London Business School and Wits.

Ching-In Chen is a genderqueer Chinese American hybrid writer, community organizer and teacher. They are author of *The Heart's Traffic* and *recombinant* (winner of the 2018 Lambda Literary Award for Transgender Poetry) as well as the chapbooks *to make black paper sing* and *Kundiman for Kin :: Information Retrieval for Monsters* (Finalist for the Leslie Scalapino Award). Chen is also co-editor of *The Revolution Starts at Home: Confronting Intimate Violence Within Activist Communities* and *Here Is a Pen: an Anthology of West Coast Kundiman Poets*. They have received fellowships from Kundiman, Lambda, Watering Hole, Can Serrat and Imagining America and are a part of Macondo and Voices of Our Nations Arts Foundation writing communities. They are currently an Assistant Professor in the School of Interdisciplinary Arts and Sciences and the MFA in Creative Writing and Poetics at the University of Washington Bothell. Find out more at chinginchen.com

Ellen Huang (she/her) has played both a demon and Jesus Christ (in separate performances). She holds BA in Writing + Theatre minor from Point Loma Nazarene University. Her poem "Aromantic Jesus" (*miniskirt magazine*) has been nominated for *Best of the Net*, and her poem "Sea Witch from the Deep" (Apparition Lit) was a nominee for Rhysling Awards for Best Sci-Fi/Fantasy Long Poem. Ellen reads for *Whale Road Review* and is published/forthcoming in 100+ venues including: *Moonchild Magazine, From the Farther Trees, Sword & Kettle Press, Not Deer Magazine, Wrongdoing Magazine, Lumiere Review, Lucent Dreaming, Gingerbread House Lit, Next Door Villain, horse egg literary*, and elsewhere. Occasionally, she writes spiritual reflections on movies at http://worrydollsandfloatinglights.wordpress.com. Currently, she is working on a fairy tale chapbook and an ace horror anthology in her tower made of way too many books—which she still hasn't learned how to shrink.

Elsa Valmidiano is the author of *We Are No Longer Babaylan*, her debut essay collection from New Rivers Press. She is a recipient of their Editors' Choice selection from their 2018 Many Voices Project competition in Prose. Her work has appeared in *Cosmonauts Avenue, Anomaly, Cherry Tree, Marías at Sampaguitas, Canthius, Poetry Northwest, Hairstreak Butterfly Review*, among many others, as well as anthologies such as *What God Is Honored Here?, Walang Hiya*, and *Loon Magic and Other Night Sounds*. Elsa is an alum of the DISQUIET International Literary Program in Lisbon and Summer Literary Seminars hosted in Tbilisi. She holds an MFA in Creative Writing from Mills College and has performed numerous readings. She has been nominated for *Best of the Net* and a Pushcart Prize. On her website, slicingtomatoes.com, Elsa curates a directory of Pinay visual artists of the Philippine Diaspora which she showcases alongside her poetry and prose.

féi hernandez (b.1993 Chihuahua, Mexico) is a trans, Inglewood-raised, formerly undocumented immigrant artist, writer, healer. They have been published in *POETRY, Pank Magazine, Oxford Review of Books, Frontier Poetry, The Breakbeat Poets Vol. 4: LatiNext,* amongst others. They are a Define American Fellow for 2021 and are currently the Board President of Gender Justice Los Angeles. féi is the author of the full-length poetry collection *Hood Criatura* (Sundress Publications 2020) which was on NPR's Best Books of 2020. féi collects Pokémon plushies.

Dr. Grisel Y. Acosta is a full professor at the City University of New York-BCC, and the daughter of Colombian and Cuban immigrants. She is the author of *Things to Pack on the Way to Everywhere*, a 2020 finalist for the Andrés Montoya Poetry Prize, and the editor of the Routledge anthology, *Latina Outsiders Remaking Latina Identity*. Other select work can be found in *Best American Poetry, The Baffler, The Acentos Review, Paterson Literary Review, Celebrating 20 Years of Black Girlhood: The Lauryn Hill Reader*, and is forthcoming in *Speculative Fiction for Dreamers: A Latinx Anthology* and *The Future of Black: Afrofuturism, Black Comics, and Superhero Poetry*. She is a Geraldine Dodge Foundation Poet, a Macondo Fellow, and the Creative Writing Editor of Chicana/Latina Studies Journal.

Gustavo Barahona-López is a writer and educator from Richmond, California. In his writing, Barahona-López draws from his experience growing up as the son of Mexican immigrants. His micro-chapbook *Where Will the Children Play?* was part of the Ghost City Press 2020 Summer Series. He was a finalist for the 2021 Quarterly West poetry prize. A member of the Writer's Grotto and a VONA alum, Barahona-López's work can be found or is forthcoming in *Iron Horse Literary Review, Puerto del Sol, The Acentos Review, Apogee Journal, Hayden's Ferry Review*, among other publications.

Hannu Afere is an author, visual artist and scientist whose work has appeared in *Former People, Praxis, Omenana* and other publications. His first book of poetry, *Digital Ṣìgìdì*, was released in 2020. Presently, he is the Editor-in-Chief of the Anthology of Contemporary West African Poetry (8th House Publishing, Montréal). His second book of poetry *Harmattan Wolf,* as well as his animated Sci Fi series *Black,* will be out in October 2021. He is a devoted student of all things spiritual and arcane. His social media handles are @HannuAfere on Twitter and Instagram.

Jamal Hodge is a multi-award-winning film director and writer. He is an active member of The HWA and The SFPA, being nominated for a 2021 Rhysling Award for his Poem "Fermi's Spaceship." His screenplay *Mourning Meal* has won 5 awards (including best short screenplay at the NYC Horror Film Festival, 2018). He is currently devising devious worlds to be explored in his first novel and poetry collection. Find more at writerhodge.com.

Jenna Le (jennalewriting.com) is a daughter of Vietnamese refugees who was born and raised in Minnesota. She is a New York City-based physician and the author of two poetry collections, *Six Rivers* (NYQ Books, 2011) and *A History of the Cetacean American Diaspora* (Indolent Books, 2018), the latter of which was an Elgin Awards second place winner. Her poems have appeared in *AGNI, Denver Quarterly, Los Angeles Review, Massachusetts Review, Michigan Quarterly Review, Pleiades, Poet Lore, Verse Daily, West Branch*, and elsewhere.

Jennifer Perrine is the author of four award-winning books of poetry: *Again, The Body Is No Machine, In the Human Zoo*, and *No Confession, No Mass*. Their recent short stories and essays appear in *Buckman Journal* and *The Gay & Lesbian Review*. Perrine lives in Portland, Oregon, where they co-host the Incite: Queer Writers Read series, teach creative writing to youth and adults, and serve as a diversity, equity, inclusion, and justice (DEIJ) consultant. To learn more visit, jenniferperrine.org.

KL Lyons is a poet from Tulsa, Oklahoma and a citizen of the Muscogee Nation. Her work has previously appeared in *Anomaly, Tulsa Review* and *Eye to the Telescope*. You can find her in your kitchen, drinking the last of your coffee, or on Twitter as @dystopialloon.

Laura Villareal earned her MFA from Rutgers University-Newark. She has received fellowships from the Stadler Center for Poetry and Literary Arts, National Book Critics Circle, and The Highlights Foundation. Her writing has appeared in *AGNI, Guernica, Black Warrior Review*, and elsewhere. She is the author of *Girl's Guide to Leaving* (University of Wisconsin Press, 2022).

Lee Murray is a multi-award-winning author-editor from Aotearoa-New Zealand (Sir Julius Vogel, Australian Shadows) and a double Bram Stoker Award®-winner. A third-generation Chinese New Zealander, she is an NZSA Honorary Literary Fellow, and the Grimshaw Sargeson Fellow for 2021 for her narrative prose-poetry work *Fox Spirit on a Distant Cloud*. Her debut poetry collection, *Tortured Willows*, a collaboration with Christina Sng, Angela Yuriko Smith, and Geneve Flynn, is forthcoming from Yuriko Publishing. Read more at leemurray.info.

Lucy Zhang writes, codes and watches anime. Her work has appeared in *The Portland Review, The Suburban Review, Orca, Milk Candy Review*, and elsewhere, and is anthologized in *Best Microfiction 2021* and *Best Small Fictions 2021*. She edits for *Barren Magazine, Heavy Feather Review* and *Pithead Chapel*. Find her at kowaretasekai.wordpress.com or on Twitter @Dango_Ramen.

Matthew E. Henry (MEH) is the author of the poetry chapbooks *Teaching While Black* (Main Street Rag, 2020) and *Dust & Ashes* (Californios Press, 2020), and his full-length collection, *the Colored page*, is forthcoming from Sundress Publications. The Editor-in-Chief of *The Weight Journal*, MEH's recent poetry and prose is appearing or forthcoming in *Poetry East, Bending Genres, Lucky Jefferson, Massachusetts Review, New York Quarterly, Ploughshares, Porcupine Literary*, and *Shenandoah*. MEH's an educator who received his MFA, yet continued to spend money he didn't have completing an MA in theology and a PhD in education. You can find him at www.MEHPoeting.com writing about education, race, religion, and burning oppressive systems to the ground.

Minoti Vaishnav is a South Asian author, poet and film and television writer who has produced content for NatGeo, Netflix, Discovery Channel and History Channel, and has written for The Equalizer on CBS. Her poetry and fiction has been published in eight publications in 2021 alone, including anthologies like *Tales from Alternate Earths Vol. 3, A Collection of Children's Stories* and *Ernest Lived and other Historical Fiction Stories* to name a few. She is an alumna of the ViacomCBS Writers Mentoring Program and holds a masters degree in creative writing from the University of Oxford.

Owólabi Aboyade (William Copeland) is a father, an MC, writer, editor, organizer, facilitator and a priest (Isese) from Detroit. Owólabi crafts portals to holistic liberation via sharing analysis, creative nonfiction, poems, and short stories in publications such as

Geez Magazine, the Audubon Magazine, Drumvoices ReVue, Riverwise Magazine, Hood Communist. He is also the co-creator of *Bullet*Train*, a digital zine chronicling Detroit's revolutionary culture in 2020. He has received recognition by the Science Fiction Poetry Association and the Odd Contest. Owólabi is a co-founder of Relentless Bodies, a Detroit-based creative disability and healing justice collective, and a lover of commas, and crystals too.

Quincy Scott Jones is an educator and author of two books of poetry: *The T-Bone Series* (Whirlwind Press, 2009) and *How to Kill Yourself Instead of Your Children* (C&R Press, 2021). His work has appeared in the *African American Review, The North American Review, the Bellingham Review, Love Jawns: A Mixtape,* and *The Feminist Wire* as well as anthologies *Resisting Arrest: Poems to Stretch the Sky, COVID Chronicles: A Comics Anthology, Black Lives Have Always Mattered: A Collection of Essays, Poems, and Personal Narratives* and *Drawn to Marvel: Poems from the Comic Books.* With Nina Sharma he co-curates "Blackshop", a column that thinks about allyship between BIPOC artists. His graphic narrative, >*Black Nerd*<, is in the works.

Russell Nichols is a speculative fiction writer and endangered journalist. Raised in Richmond, California, he got rid of all his stuff in 2011 to live out of a backpack with his wife, vagabonding around the world ever since. Look for him at russellnichols.com.

Shagufta Mulla, DVM is an artist, emerging poet & writer, and an Amherst Writers & Artists workshop facilitator. Her poetry has appeared in *ARC Journal, Orangepeel,* and *Blood Moon Journal.* Her art has been featured in *ARC Journal* and is forthcoming in *Opia.* Poems and paintings are containers for her to explore the effects of childhood emotional trauma, veterinary trauma, and healing. She holds a DVM from Colorado State University and a BS from the University of Arizona. Shagufta lives in Independence, OR and she can be found on Instagram @s.mulla.dvm.

Shanta Lee Gander's work has been featured in many publications. She is the 2020 recipient of the Arthur Williams Award for Meritorious Service to the Arts and 2020 and named as Diode Editions full-length book contest winner for her debut poetry compilation,

GHETTOCLAUSTROPHOBIA: Dreamin of Mama While Trying to Speak Woman in Woke Tongues (June 2021). Shanta Lee gives lectures on the life of Lucy Terry Prince as a member of the Vermont and New Hampshire Humanities Council Speakers Bureaus. She is the 2020 gubernatorial appointee to their board of directors. To see her photography and writing, visit Shantaleegander.com

Uche Ogbuji, more properly Úchèńnà Ogbújí, fell into writing poetry and performing spoken word while studying engineering at Nsukka, in his native Nigeria. His chapbook, *Ndewo, Colorado* (Aldrich Press), is a Colorado Book Award Winner. His forthcoming book, *Ńchéfù Road* is winner of the Christopher Smart Prize in the UK. Work published worldwide fuses Igbo culture, European classicism, American Mountain West settings, Hip-Hop and afrofuturism. He's settled in Colorado after much world wandering.

Vivian Faith Prescott was born and raised on the island of Ḵaachx̱aana.áak'w, Wrangell, Alaska, in the Alexander Archipelago where she lives and writes at Mickey's Fishcamp near Ḵeishangita.aan, Red Alder Head Village. She's Sámi American (Indigenous Sámi diaspora) and a member of the Pacific Sámi Searvi, plus a founding member of Community Roots, the first LGBTQIA group on the island. She's the author of two full-length poetry collections, five chapbooks, and a short story collection. Her poetry has been translated into the North Sámi language in Sapmi (Scandinavia) and appears in the Sámi language journal *Sámis Nuvtta*. Her foodoir, *My Father's Smokehouse*, is forthcoming from West Margin Press/ Alaska Northwest Books in 2022, as well as a full-length poetry collection from the University of Alaska Press, Alaska Literary Series: *Old Woman With Berries in Her Lap*, poems that explore the Sámi diaspora.

Newark, NJ native **Ysabel Y. González** received her BA from Rutgers University, an MFA in Poetry from Drew University and works as the Assistant Director for the Poetry Program at the Geraldine R. Dodge Foundation. Ysabel has received invitations to attend VONA, Tin House, Ashbery Home School and BOAAT Press workshops. She's a CantoMundo Fellow and has been published in *Tinderbox Journal; Anomaly; Vinyl; Waxwing Literary Journal*, and others. She is a Pushcart Prize nominee and the author of *Wild Invocations* (Get Fresh Books, 2019). You can read more at ysabelgonzalez.com.

Zeenat Khan is an Indian poet of 20. She is doing her under-graduation in English Literature from Vivekananda College, Delhi University. Her poems and artworks appear or are forthcoming in *Haiku Foundation, Borderless Journal, Café Dissensus, Harbinger Asylum, Hakara Journal, Red River* and many international anthologies. In 2020, she was awarded World Architectural Poetry Award. Currently, she is working with *The Sunflower Collective* and *The Quiver Review* as a part of the editorial and advisory board.

About the Editor

Akua Lezli Hope is a creator and wisdom seeker who uses sound, words, fiber, glass, metal, and wire to create poems, patterns, stories, music, sculpture, adornments, peace, and change. She wrote her first speculative poems in the sixth grade and has been in print every year since 1974. She is published in numerous literary magazines and national anthologies including the award winning first anthology of black science fiction, *Dark Matter*.

A third generation, African Caribbean New Yorker, her honors include the National Endowment of the Arts fellowship, two New York Foundation of the Arts fellowships, a SFPA award, several Rhysling and Pushcart Prize nominations, among many other scholarships, grants and honors. She twice won Rattle's Poets Respond. Her first collection, *EMBOUCHURE, Poems on Jazz and Other Musics*, won the Writer's Digest book award. A Cave Canem fellow, her collection, *THEM GONE*, was published in 2018. She launched Speculative Sundays, an online poetry reading series in 2020. Her micro-chapbook of scifaiku, *Stratospherics*, is in the Quarantine Public Library. A paraplegic, she founded a paratransit nonprofit.

Her speculative poetry chapbook, *Otherwheres* (ArtFarm Press 2020), is nominated for a 2021 Elgin award. She is editor of *Eye to The Telescope 42, The Sea*. An avid hand papermaker and crochet designer with over 130 patterns published, she exhibits her artwork regularly. She sings songs from her favorite anime in Japanese, practices her soprano saxophone, cajoles an indifferent cat and prays for the cessation of suffering for all sentience.

Other Anthologies by Sundress Publications

The Familiar Wild: On Dogs & Poetry
Edited by Ruth Awad and Rachel Mennies

Not Somewhere Else But Here: A Contemporary Anthology of Women & Place
Edited by Erin Elizabeth Smith and T.A. Noonan

Till the Tide: An Anthology of Mermaid Poetry
Edited by Trista Edwards

Gathered: Contemporary Quaker Poets
Edited by Nick McRae

www.ingramcontent.com/pod-product-compliance
Lightning Source LLC
Chambersburg PA
CBHW080717020726
47501CB00010B/2461